Amazing Animal Groups

A family of gorillas lives in a mountain forest in Africa.

by Suzanne Venino

BOOKS FOR YOUNG EXPLORERS
NATIONAL GEOGRAPHIC SOCIETY

African elephants crowd together in a circle
to guard their young from danger.
Suddenly, a huge female elephant charges!
She defends the group by frightening away enemies.
Elephants live in groups called herds.
Living in groups helps animals in different ways.

A herd of elephants gathers at a water hole. The elephants
suck water into their trunks and squirt it into their mouths.
Nearby, two young elephants help each other take a mud bath.
Mud protects their tender skin from the hot sun and from insects.
The herd may travel many miles to the next water hole.

In Africa, gorillas rest together in a forest. The adult members
of the group watch over the young ones as they play.
Gorillas may look fierce, but they are really gentle and shy.
They spend most of their time looking for food or resting.

While the adults rest,
the young gorillas
chew on twigs
and branches.

In a tree, a mother gorilla
and her baby build a nest
where they can take a nap.
The young gorilla learns
by watching its mother.
Another baby plays
on the ground.
If it is hurt or scared,
it runs to its mother.
An older gorilla
beats his chest as if to say
to the others, "Look at me.
I'm big and strong!"

Zebras live in large herds on the hot, flat plains of Africa.
They usually stay near a river or a water hole.
Living together helps these striped animals protect themselves.
While some members of the herd take a drink,
others keep a sharp lookout for lions or other enemies.

Something has frightened these zebras.
Perhaps they heard a noise or smelled a lion.
The zebras scramble out of the water.
The herd then gallops away to escape danger.

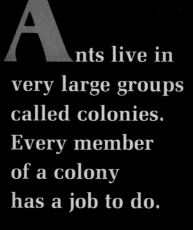

Ants live in very large groups called colonies. Every member of a colony has a job to do.

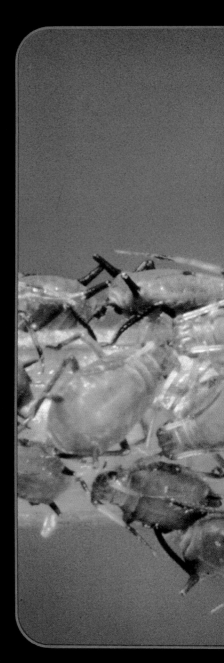

Ants called leaf-cutters take bits of leaves back to their nest. Hundreds of army ants march over fallen branches. Some of them join together to make a bridge. Others carry young ants to a new nest. The young are white and do not yet look like adults. By stroking tiny insects called aphids, a big black ant gathers sweet juice from them. The ant will share the juice with its colony.

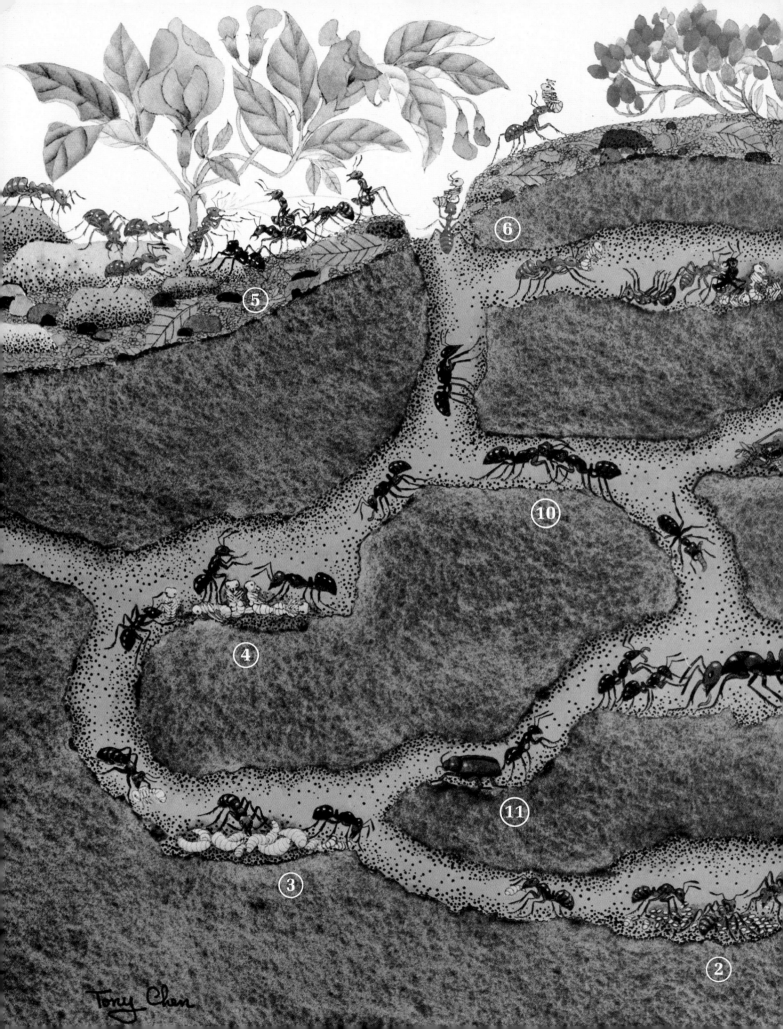

This painting shows the nest of some black ants. It is underground. Match the numbers on the painting with the numbers below to find out what the ants are doing.

1. The queen ant lays many eggs.
2. Worker ants lick the eggs clean.
3. Workers feed young ants, called larvae. The larvae will change into pupae.
4. Workers care for pupae, which will change into adult ants.
5. Red ants attack the black ants.
6. Red ants carry off the young of black ants to keep as slaves.
7. Ants bring a dead grasshopper into the nest for food.
8. Ants get juice from aphids.
9. Food is stored in a special room.
10. Two ants feed each other.
11. A beetle comes into the nest.
12. Workers dig a new tunnel.

Penguins squeal and squawk as they greet one another.
These large birds have wings but do not fly. They use their wings
as flippers to swim in the ocean near the South Pole.
A parade of penguins heads down to the ocean to fish for food.
The birds look like big wind-up toys as they waddle across the snow.
Swoosh! A penguin dives into the icy cold water for a swim.

17

Most of the time penguins
live in small groups in the sea.
Once a year they gather
in huge numbers on land
to mate and to have their young.
Two penguins warn another one
to keep away from their nest.
The female penguin lays
an egg in a nest of stones.

When the chick hatches
from the egg, both parents
help feed it and care for it.
Penguin chicks grow quickly.
In about six months,
they start to shed
their fluffy brown feathers and
grow black and white ones.

A large school of fish swims through the ocean. Living in schools helps protect fish from enemies. So many fish swimming together may confuse a larger fish if it tries to catch one of them.

White pelicans leave their nests to find food. Working together, these big birds flap their wings on the water to stir up fish. Then the pelicans open their bills and scoop the fish from the sea.

A hungry young pelican gets fish by poking its head into the pouch below its mother's bill.

A family of prairie dogs
sits in the warm sunshine.
Standing up, one nibbles a weed.
Other prairie dogs tumble and play.
These small, furry animals live
in large groups called towns.
They dig holes and tunnels to build
underground homes, or burrows.

Prairie dogs climb out of their burrow.
They look and listen for signs of danger.
The bison will not bother them.
But if a prairie dog spots an enemy,
it barks a warning to the others,
and they all scamper back underground.

Ow-ooo! A wolf calls to other wolves with a long howl. Wolves live together in groups called packs. When hunting for food, a pack follows its leader, an older and stronger wolf.

A member of a pack licks
the lead wolf in the mouth
when they meet.
This is one way that
wolves show respect
for their leaders.

Thick fur keeps a wolf
warm as it rests
in the cold winter snow.

A huge male sea lion
nuzzles his mate. Their young pup
wants some attention, too.
Once a year sea lions
gather on land in large groups
to mate and to have their young.
Many other kinds of animals
live together all the time.
As you have seen, animals live
in groups for different reasons.
Can you name some of them?

Published by The National Geographic Society
Gilbert M. Grosvenor, *President;* Melvin M. Payne, *Chairman of the Board;*
Owen R. Anderson, *Executive Vice President;* Robert L. Breeden, *Vice President,*
Publications and Educational Media

Prepared by The Special Publications Division
Donald J. Crump, *Director*
Philip B. Silcott, *Associate Director*
William L. Allen, William R. Gray, *Assistant Directors*

Staff for this Book
Margery G. Dunn, *Managing Editor*
John Agnone, *Picture Editor*
Marianne R. Koszorus, *Art Director*
Walton Ferrell, *Researcher*
Katheryn M. Slocum, *Illustrations Assistant*

Engraving, Printing, and Product Manufacture
Robert W. Messer, *Manager*
George V. White, *Production Manager*
David V. Showers, *Production Project Manager*
Mark R. Dunlevy, Richard A. McClure, Raja D. Murshed, Christine A. Roberts, Gregory Storer, *Assistant Production Managers*
Mary A. Bennett, Katherine H. Donohue, *Production Staff Assistants*

Debra A. Antonini, Nancy F. Berry, Pamela A. Black, Nettie Burke, Jane H. Buxton, Claire M. Doig, Rosamund Garner, Victoria
   D. Garrett, Virginia A. McCoy, Cleo Petroff, Victoria I. Piscopo, Tammy Presley, Carol A. Rocheleau, Jenny Takacs, *Staff Assistants*

Consultants
Lila Bishop, Dr. Glenn O. Blough, Karen O. Strimple, *Educational Consultants*
Lynda Ehrlich, *Reading Consultant*
Dr. David R. Smith, Systematic Entomology Laboratory, USDA, *Scientific Consultant*

Illustrations Credits
Jen and Des Bartlett (cover, 16, 16-17, 19); Robert M. Campbell (1, 8, 9 lower right); Leonard Lee Rue III (2-3 upper); Oria and Iain
Douglas-Hamilton (2-3 lower); Tom Brakefield (4, 10-11); Rick Weyerhaeuser (5 upper); Thomas Nebbia (5 lower, 11 upper); Peter
Veit (6-7); Amy Vedder (7); Alan Root (9 upper); Dian Fossey (9 lower left); Helen and Frank Schreider (11 lower); Oxford
Scientific Films (12 upper, 12 center); Rudolf Freund, Photo Researchers (12 lower); J.A.L. Cooke (12-13); Tony Chen (14-15);
Robert W. Madden, Photo Quest (17 lower left, 18 lower left, 18 lower right); David H. Thompson (17 lower right, 18 upper); David
Doubilet (20-21); Jim Brandenburg (22-23, 24, 24-25, 25 upper, 25 lower left, 25 lower right, 26 upper, 26 lower, 28-29, 29 upper,
29 lower); Harry Engels, ANIMALS ANIMALS (23); © Walt Disney Productions (26-27); Dieter Blum, Peter Arnold (30-31);
National Geographic Photographer Bruce Dale (32).

Library of Congress CIP Data
Venino, Suzanne.
   Amazing animal groups.

(Books for young explorers)
   Summary: Describes the behavior of animals that live in large social groups, including elephants, zebras, gorillas, wolves, prairie dogs, fishes, ants, and penguins.
   1. Animal societies—Juvenile literature. [1. Animal societies. 2. Animals—Habits and behavior] I. National Geographic Society (U. S.) II. Title. III. Series.
QL775.A53   591.5'24   81-47743
ISBN 0-87044-402-6 (regular binding)   AACR2
ISBN 0-87044-407-7 (library binding)

**Walruses splash in the sea.
Long teeth, called tusks,
grow from their mouths.
These animals live in big
herds near the North Pole.**

Cover: **King penguins
gather at a nesting place
called a rookery.**